Published 1986 by Temps de Pose editions
38, rue de la République
27500 Pont-Audemer. France
Exclusive distribution for India and Nepal by UBS Publishers' Distributors Ltd. New-Delhi
© Copyright 1986 photographs and captions : Pierre TOUTAIN
© Copyright 1986 text : Michel GOTIN
ISBN - 0-948075-19-8 english edition
ISBN 2-906063-00-2 french edition

Collection DESTINATION

NEPAL

**Photographs
Pierre TOUTAIN**

Text
Michel GOTIN

 UBSPD

UBS Publishers' Distributors Ltd.
5 Ansari Road, New Delhi-110002
Branches: New Delhi ● Bombay ● Bangalore ● Madras
Calcutta ● Patna ● Kanpur

The roof of the world

The Himalayas have been the refuge of the Gods since the dawn of time.

An intimate God

This statue represents Vishnu Narayana lying on the eternal serpent Ananta floating on the primeval ocean symbolised by the water-tank.

At home

A family Newar, the original settlers in the Kathmandu valley who come from a long line of superb artists.

9

the kingdom of the Gods

Nepal : a magic name, a magical land. As legend tells us, it is the seat of the Gods, sanctuary of holy men, homeland of spiritual freedom. It is also a land of demons and sorcery. With its unchanging faith and twin-traditions of Hinduism and Buddhism it leaves an indelible impression on those who take the time to explore its character.

On the appointed day, at the very dawn of time, the Gods came down to Earth from the Heavens. And they chose the roof of the world, the snow-capped peaks of Nepal encircling Sagarmatha — Mount Everest — at over 29000 feet the highest point on earth.

From these heights they kept watch over Man. Annapurna, the beautiful Goddess of Plenty, settled on one of the loftiest peaks. She gave it her name and bestowed her bounty on those dwelling in the valley below. The people of Pokhara — a town known today as a base for many treks into the mountains — were especially favoured, and their plentiful harvests were famed throughout the land. Shiva, one of the Gods making up the Hindu Trinity, and his loyal wife Parvati, chose Gauri Shankar, while their son, Ganesh, whose elephant-featured image is seen and revered every-where as the benificent protector of the home, made Ganesh Himal his abode. Many centuries later, in an age when the sky still merged with the sea, the valley of Kathmandu was but a vast lake, reflecting only the distant, proud peaks, symbols of radiant purity. The mythical serpent Naga Karkotaka, lord of the waves and the rain, ruled over this liquid world, when one moonlit night, a sage named Bipaswi cast into the lake a lotus seed. In less than a year there appeared a flower, a magnificent bloom which shone with a brilliance never before seen. From its centre emerged the first image of Buddha — Swayambhu — the God born of himself. The patriarch Manjushri, arriving from China with other believers, decided to erect on this spot a *stupa,* an immense temple whose grandeur reflected the significance of the event. Drawing his magic sword, symbol of wisdom, he struck the mountainside with on single, almighty blow. From this wound the waters gushed out through the gorge of Chobar, whose sheer sides even today testify to the terrible force of the blow.

Thus came into being the wondrous Stupa of Swayambhunath and the town of Kathmandu, known of old as the legendary Kantipur, capital of a fabled land that is Nepal.

A chilly dawn at Kirtipur.

When the street becomes a temple...

*Kirtipur, one of the oldest villages
of the Kathmandu valley,
built by king Shiva Deva
in the twelfth century.*

Ganesh the benevolent

Plump, mischievious and smiling, Ganesh combines strentgh with guile and protects against evil spirits.

The subtle charm of Patan.

*The colour red is everywhere,
standing for vitality,
passion and life itself.*

*This sick Brahman belongs
to the highest caste.*

between India and Tibet

Nepal has won my heart. Like all those who arrive from India, by air from Delhi, in the early hours of the morning, I was captivated by the sight of the incredible mountain chain which gradually spread from the horizon to completely fill the view from the windows on the left side of the plane.

It appeared at first as a gigantic rocky mass whose dark outline could scarcely be made out against a sky still studded with thousands of glittering stars. Suddenly the sun burst forth and transformed this landscape of shadows ; out of the peaks, pinnacles and ridges were conjured images of crystal palaces, holy sanctuaries and glorious battlefields.

At that moment, the incredible, almost surreal beauty of the scene explained and totally justified all the risks and sacrifices of the mountaineers who assemble here from all over the world. Year after year they set off to conquer the peaks, as though drawn by some enigmatic lover.

The wing of the aeroplane tilts and the view on both sides is of the tall, pointed hills carved into terraces, intersected by small, deep valleys with their straight-running streams whose source is in the Himalayas. Some of these are sacred, like the sluggish Bagmati that crosses Kathmandu, and threads its way through countryside dominated by the mountains of Siwalik and the region of Mahabharat, before at last achieving the supreme consecration by flowing into that most sacred river of all, the Ganges.

Hilltops are crowned with small temples. Pale green patches of ripening corn contrast with darker, arc-shaped outlines of paddyfields, then yield to the gentle plains streaked with the brilliant yellow fields of mustard in flower.

Tiny barren plateaux, whose parched red earth has been scattered by the wind, shelter the often ancient villages. The houses, made of ashlar or ochre clay, with only the first floor whitewashed, reveal the ethnic origins of the population. Thatched roofs are decorated with dried maize, buffalo languish in the shade, black pigs rush around. At the last minute, just as the morning mist is settling on the valley, a sudden blaze of light illuminates the gilded dome of the 2000 years old Swayambhunath. The centuries telescope as the plane touches down on the runway at Tribuhan, cutting a passage through the swirling smoke that rises up from funeral pyres along the ghats of Pashupatinath. The stars have vanished and the rising sun brings the mist. Kathmandu shivers in the early morning beneath its blanket of moisture, still captive to the dreams and charms of the night.

This huge statue dating from the seventeenth century represents Khala Bhairava, God of destruction.
He is one of the forms of Shiva.

*This young Newar girl is destined
to be the living goddess,
the Kumari.*

*Ganesh,
the elephant-headed God.*

It is the hour of first prayers and ablutions. Young girls bend beneath a low stone lintel with the sign of Ganesh at its centre. Each one carries a brass vessel for the household water. Light-hearted, graceful and smiling, their saris draped around their bodies and framing their faces to emphasise their big dark eyes lined with kohl, they linger for a moment at a statue of Vishnu. With their thumbs they deftly retouch the small round *tilaka* mark that they wear on their foreheads, with a red paste made of cinnabar, clay, rice and flower petals. Children play at the edge of one of the communal water tanks, water spurts from the mouth of a roaring brass dragon. Wisps of mist rise from a drinking trough and mingle with the steamy breath from the moist, warm muzzles of the cattle wandering in search of food.

Sheer perfection

Statue and sculpture are of rare finesse

The clanking of heavy cast-iron catches, the clattering of shutters being opened, and the dry cracking sound of mats being unrolled and shaken, echo round the streets. Fires are lit under cauldrons and under the pans which are used for frying breads. Hairdressers warm their fingers over red embers on an earthenware saucer. Sitting on the bottom steps of a pagoda, half a dozen tailors carefully clean the chrome wheels of their old sewing machines. In front of them are piles of bobbins with their threads of multicoloured silks, and gold sashes.

Rickshaw drivers tap gently on the painted hoods of their vehicles to shake off drops of dew. At the ancient city gates a throng of porters gathers. They carry all manner of things in the nets and on the plates that are suspended from bamboo rods arched across their shoulders. Peasants arrive at the open air markets with their big boxes of red radishes, turnips, cabbages and oranges. Their light step contrasts sharply with the slow shuffle of a line of women, children and old people, their eyes fixed on the track. They carry packs of wood on their backs attached to cloth or leather straps tied around their heads. They have often travelled a great distance to sell their bundles of firewood for just twenty-five rupees each. Some of the women carry unweaned infants whose sleeping mouths seek out their mothers' milk.

Waves of Chinese-made bicycles try to clear a path for themselves with much ringing of bells. In enormous saddle bags, chickens with their legs tied, squawk half-heartedly. Goats and ducks fight over a pool of water where ragged infants are playing, their feet squeezed into little rubber boots.

Once the mist has dispersed and the patches of moisture have yielded to the sun's rays, the crowd comes to life as though touched by a magic wand. All races are represented and co-exist happily, their ethnic origins identifiable by their eyes, the shape of their cheekbones and their colouring, as well as by their clothes and jewellery. Business is often done in Nepalese, the official language, close to Hindi and derived from Sanscrit. But there are no fewer than thirty-six other languages and dialects in current usage amongst a population of over sixteen million.

The finest collections of tanka can be found at Bhagdaon. In this one the artist has painted a mandala which represents the universe as it is conceived in Buddhism and Tantra.

Even for hardened mountain people,
every crossing of a rope-bridge
has its share of danger.

*In the foothills of the himalayas
a village is caught
in the onslaught
of heavy storm clouds
from the plains
of the Ganges.*

Between heaven and earth

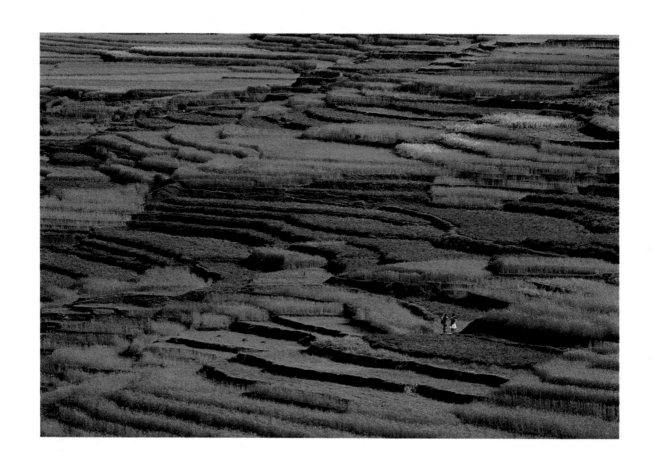

*Symbol of plenty,
enlightenment and knowledge,
handfuls of rice are
thrown at every festival
to honour the Gods.*

Initiation

In rural areas sacred writings are used to teach children to read and write.

Children of the Kathmandu valley.

*A way of life where religious belief
is inseparable from
everyday life.*

Golden grass

Yellow fields of mustard provide the last splash of colour before the monsoon.

Petrified waterfalls

The hills of Nagarkot are terraced to facilitate cultivation and harvesting.

the legendary Kathmandu

I love Kathmandu, where legends worthy of the Thousand and One Nights overlap with history, and the Middle Ages still linger, gently resisting the advances of the modern world. You can get around Kathmandu on foot or perhaps hire a bicycle. To go further afield, there are always rickshaws and the indescribable three and four wheeled taxis, wobbly and overloaded, that struggle valiantly to cut a path, with much hooting, stopping and starting.

What I love best is to wander around with no other purpose than to observe the people, perhaps to come upon an old fountain or a monument, hidden in a little courtyard, to see children playing, craftsmen at work, and of course to stop a while at one of the many temples that mark out the area of the old city.

In the old Newar quarter, there is still an atmosphere of adventure so strong that it takes little imagination to relive the great era of trade with China, Tibet and India.

From here were taken salt, oil, precious stones, weapons and carpets. The finest saris edgeg in gold arrived with the caravans twice a year. It was the time for choosing the sari of the young bride, for buying one of the finely sculpted ivory statuettes, or for admiring a bronze Buddha. Almost nothing has changed. These old settlements are still today self-administrating communities ; people still gather at the fountains to exchange gossip.

The temple bells ring out as the worshippers pass, and the prayer wheels turn constantly, pushed by eager, faithful hands. Om Mani Padme Hum — to the Greater Glory of God — that is the prayer, that the message inscribed three times on the bronze rollers, turning untiringly, while a couple of paces away street sellers shake out saris in the breeze. Makhan Tole is awash with colour, the finest gold contrasting with the brightest red, white with blue. Great piles of cloth are rolled and unrolled, and the animated ritual of haggling begins. The customer examines the wares, argues over the price, then walks off empty handed and cross, only to return smiling, called back at the last moment. Further on stands a statue, a dancing figure with six arms. With its torch, its death's-heads and its sword it is an awe-inspiring sight. It is Kal Bhairava before whom oaths are

Sustained by their faith, the Sadhu have abandoned all worldly possessions. These mystics set out on their pilgrimages with only a modest bundle containing religious articles and texts.

sworn — perjurers beware ! A *tilbu,* a tiny little Tibetan bell, tinkles in my ear. I turn to face a Tibetan with a beaming smile framed by a long moustache. He offers me the bell to examine. It is beautiful, has a purity of tone and is probably antique. If it is for sale, it is only because of the forthcoming New Year celebrations at Bodhnath, the biggest sanctuary for Tibetans in exile in Nepal. The reunion will be expensive, so, since to bargain under such circumstances would cause offence, I take it without arguing over the price, so as never to forget that haunting, sacred air.

Swept along by a surge of street hawkers, and following tight groups of pilgrims who have come on foot from India, I find myself in Durbar Square. Within these royal and ancient walls there are more than fifty shrines, palaces and monuments, which, along with the temples at the rival cities of Patan and Bhaktapur, give a vivid and comprehensive impression of the glory and splendour of bygone days.

After the narrow little streets where light is filtered through objects hanging from windows and balconies, the full sunlight is blinding as it strikes the tall pillars, monumental doorways, strange statues, gilded sculptures and immense stairways leading to the galleries of the giant pagodas. It is a world apart, proud, magnificent and oppressive, where if you scratch the gold you may uncover blood — the blood of sacrifice and of the old internal wars and battles of succession.

There you will find the ancient palace of the Malla kings, the temple of Shiva and Parvati, the grandiose pagoda of Taleju with its three bronze roofs which dominate the city, and the home of the Kumari Bahal, the living Goddess still honoured today.

The Kumari is selected from amongst young girls of the Sakya tribe who possess thirty-two distinguishing characteristics and display extraordinary composure, and she remains in office only until the onset of puberty or until her blood spills from a wound. At an awe-inspiring ceremony she is exhibited before the bloody heads of a hundred buffalo ; men dressed as demons dance around her. Once a year, during the feast of Indra Jatra, the Kumari is paraded through the city streets on a chariot decked with flowers. When her duties are over she is free to marry and has a substantial dowry, but according to legend she will bring bad luck to her future husband, and this has discouraged more than one suitor.

Far from these preoccupations, children sell souvenirs in the shade of the steps which rise in five tiers to be crowned by the triple roof of the temple of Narayan, consecrated to Vishnu, whose galleries are the setting for many holy ceremonies. With incredible mental agility they offer black market rates for any and every currency. The opposite side of the square is the preserve of the floral garland sellers, and rickshaw drivers sounding their horns at every opportunity to attract the attention of prospective customers.

Traffic circulates in all directions. Porters gasp beneath the weight of their burdens. Children play at hoopla, with marbles or with small coins. Peasants sell brightly coloured fruits, cripples beg a few rupees.

On the flat roof of the temple of Bhimsen which dominates the whole square, I feel isolated from the human throng nine stories below. A procession approaches. The motley crowd parts to make way for a golden canopy held high in the air. It moves first towards the temple of Shiva and Parvati whose sculpted busts appear at a wrought iron window, then to the large column which bears the statues of King Pratap Malla and his wife, who were responsible for the building of most of the monuments in Durbar

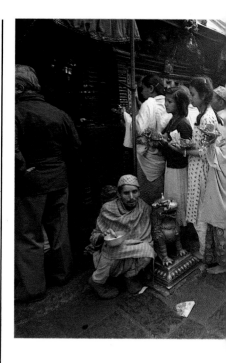

The faithful come to Kasthamandapa Square in Kathmandu to make their morning offerings at the Simba-Sattal, the Shivaic oratory.

44

Square.

A few steps from the statue of the monkey-God Hanuman, who wears a red cloak and is painted with a thick layer of cinnabar mixed with oil, a man suddenly breaks away from the little group of faithful followers which has joined the procession. In his right hand he holds a small piece of paper on which he has written his request. A stick of incense burns in his left hand. He pauses a moment, then slips his message between two loose stones before rejoining his companions who have disappeared into the courtyard of the palace guarded by two stone lions. Not for an instant do the Buddhist priests, pilgrims, Sadhu and men and women that pass in a constant stream before the temple of Jagannath raise their eyes to the erotic sculptures that adorn the beams and struts of the roof. Some of the statues are primitive works, painted in bright colours, while others are in plain wood, their poses explicit. These erotic images are to be found in many of the temples, and they do not shock : they are there to remind you that in Tantric every human act is sublimated to the will of God, to make man divine. Every gesture, every single thought have their part to play in the cosmic universe. Everything leads to God. Some tantric texts teach followers to eat meat and fish, to drink wine and to satisfy sexual desires. That is why the Sadhu sitting on the temple steps is not unduly distressed. In front of him is a bowl which will be filled by passers by. He has long hair, powdered ash on his face and a mark on his forehead. He is an ascetic who has gone about on foot since taking his vows of poverty. Never would it enter his head to demand that the erotic statues be banned, for remember we are in Nepal, land of spiritual freedom.

In front of Taleju pagoda a dog is sniffing at the dust. Its nose pressed to the ground, it whimpers before the vast door that opens for only the King, certain preachers and Hindus on the day of the feast of Durga Puja. It quivers at the smell of the blood of a thousand goats and buffalo that have been sacrificed in the middle of the square by Gurkha soldiers whose pride is in the slitting of the throats of their victims with a single stroke of the sword. The rooftops drip with gold, there is blood on the paving stones. This grand and splendid feast is not for those of a sensitive disposition. It is a ceremony that arouses feelings of fear and dread, but at the same time an immense thirst for life.

Two flute sellers play a little tune. They have dozens of flutes for sale, fixed to poles which they carry across their shoulders. An old lady beckons me to her fruit display. Children scrounge a cigarette, which they hold in the distinctive way of the country, between the first and third fingers, with both hands cupped together — one of the pleasures of Nepal. On the steps of the temple of Shiva Mandir young girls offer cotton hair ribbons for sale. Their red colour stands out in sharp contrast to the thick black hair, whose parting,in the case of married women, is also red, coloured with simrick. Their ears are pierced with four or five gold rings, and the nose is adorned with a fine jewel — the value of which is a measure on the family's financial status. They laugh and are merry. They have sold well and tomorrow is another day. Their bundles slung on a wide strap that cuts into their brows, they make their way in small groups towards one of the most beautiful monasteries in the capital — Seto Machlendranath, refuge of the God of Compassion, revered equally by Hindus and Buddhists. The way to the temple is indicated by bronze griffins. After the dimness of the covered approach, the sunlight seems dazzling in the vast court-yard surrounded by tall houses with balconies. Children play ball, heedless of the prayers rising

In the heart of the land of the Sherpa

*Activity in Namche Bazar, the capital, revolves around
international mountaineering expeditions.*

Purifying waters

Once every twelve years thousands of pilgrims make their way to Panauti to glorify Vishnu.

Built in 1708,
the temple of Nyatapola

from the gallery where a group of some twenty pilgrims sit. Metal standards point to the sky, multicoloured flags flap in the wind and plaited sashes swing from the roof.

But not all the cultural riches of Kathmandu can be so easily discovered. You need lots of patience and curiosity to go searching for the thousand secret courtyards, each one revealing a sanctuary or a little temple or perhaps just a beautiful devotional image.

Expressions of gratitude to the Gods are many and varied, and come in unexpected forms : the temple of Ugratara for instance, is mainly visited by people with eye problems, and its walls are hung with spectacles as signs of thanks.

Elsewhere a clove tree calms the misery of those with toothache : the action of driving an iron tip into the bark kills off the devil that is attacking your jaw. If by any slight chance this tried and tested procedure does not suffice, there are open-air booths nearby with dentists ever ready to attend their customers. This arrangement makes it as easy to choose a practitioner as it is to select your false teeth from a wide range displayed in large glass jars.

*In Blaktapur is
the tallest pagoda in Nepal.
In three strides Vishnu
covered the globe.*

For centuries the old town of Kathmandu remained untouched, except for the destruction caused by the 1934 earthquake which mainly affected the commercial area. You can easily spot the architectural styles that have hardly changed from the beginning to the end of the Newar rule. The first changes appeared when the Rana came to power. This period began in 1850 when Prime Minister Jung Bahadur Rana returned from a long journey to England and France, and began to introduce the western ideas of the time. The palace of Singha Durbar, built at his instigation, went far beyond what anyone could have imagined. With its seventeen internal courtyards and one thousand eight hundred rooms designed to provide fitting accommodation for the Prime Minister, his wives and his five hundred concubines, it was, it seemed, the largest residence in the world. Designed by French architects and erected in less than two years, it is eight times larger than the Palace of Versailles. But Singha Durbar is only one of the hundreds of palaces built by the Rana in the valley, albeit the most important and the most remarkable — one wing was unfortunately destroyed by fire on the day after a decree was signed forbidding drug trafficking.

*The most beautiful flowers
and the finest rice
are the special offerings
for Vishnu Narayana.*

The modern city spreads out towards the east. Here are embassies, travel agents, Japanese car dealers, administrative offices and shops selling equipment for mountaineering expeditions. At the frontier of these two worlds is New Road, the former Juddha Sadak, shopwindow of the new consumer society born on the day that King Tribhuwan returned to Kathmandu in 1951 and put an end to the reign of the Rana. The country was then opened to foreigners for the first time.

Drawn by the novelty and beauty of the place, the minimal cost of living, the lack of regulation over the growth and sale of drugs, many hippies took the road to Kathmandu. These were often the first westerners to come into contact with a people whose spirit of tolerance has never deserted them, even when faced with certain individuals whose behaviour showed an all too casual disregard for their way of life.

Hardly a trace now remains of this period, or of « Freak Street », that narrow street which became notorious the world over for its stalls, its cafés and its « useful contacts ». Perhaps the only reminder is the shadowy figure a few paces behind you who persuasively offers you hashish and opium for sale. These dealers make use of the same persistent sales technique and articulacy as the antique dealers of the area who offer, with an air of mystery and under the seal of secrecy, genuine antique statues, yellowed ivory Buddhas, silver bracelets, emerald and turquoise necklets and coral brooches. Their arguments are sometimes drowned out by loudspeakers noisily advertising the latest fashions from London, New York and Rome at tiny counters.

Posters of Hollywood stars hang alongside advertisements for airlines. Carpet dealers display at their first-floor windows, protected from the dust, the products of Tibetan craft workshops. These are usually big carpets in traditional designs, made at Jawalakel, one of the country's refugee camps which together shelter many hundreds of thousands of Tibetans.

To get to the bus station you have to go to the other side of Tundikel, the biggest military training ground in the whole of Asia, and the scene of special parades and march pasts in honour of foreign sovereigns. The bus station presents an astonishing spectacle, and the atmosphere must be much as it was in olden days as the caravans made ready to set off. Amidst clouds of dust stirred up by the buses, whole families bustle about, arguing, shouting, grumbling, chasing young goats, checking that their baggage is all there and safely packed. Destinations are announced through the distorted tones of the loudspeakers. Engines warm up and get into gear as exhausts belch out clouds of thick smoke. The mechanics, often Sikhs from India, wield heavy spanners with bold self-assurance. Ladders and baggage trolleys are in constant demand. All aboard, it is time to depart. In actual fact, the speedometer never gets beyond twenty miles per hour, except, that is, for the « night express », their prestige train. It goes really fast, and takes a mere eight hours to do the Kathmandu-Pokhara journey, a distance of a hundred and twenty-five miles !

Buddha watches over the four points of the compass.

*Groups of followers spontaneously
assemble to worship Vishnu
in this open-air temple.*

Religion of the people

To the glory of Brahma

From first light, pilgrims offer holy water to Brahma, the sun-God.

magnificent Patan

If it is true that the Emperor Ashoka built the four earthen stupas of Patan, then known as Lalitpur, it is the oldest Buddhist city in the world. A few miles south of Kathmandu and separated from the capital by the river Bagmati, Patan with its five or six hundred known historic monuments, its stately temples and palaces, its bustling shops and gaily coloured markets, is my favourite place.

Here stronger than anywhere beats the heart of the Newar civilisation. Less worried by modern ideas than its neighbour, this rural, mediaeval city has kept its atmosphere and has an air of industriousness and craftsmanship, giving it a charm of its own.

It is laid out in the shape of a wheel, and was the scene of a visitation by the « Enlightened One ». It is imbued with holiness, dignity and nobility.

Firecrackers are set off in a nearby courtyard adorned with garlands of cloth. Young girls scoop up handfuls of rice from wicker baskets and toss them towards the slowly advancing procession. Carried high in the air on a beautiful carved chair there appears an old woman, whose eyes still sparkle with life and mischief. She is wearing her finest clothes in honour of her seventy-seven years, seven months and seven days, and all the street celebrates with her, for this perfect number symbolises rebirth. After making its way through the little group of houses, the procession heads for royal Durbar Square.

The range of styles and decoration, the abundance of monuments and the complex structure of the buildings all bear witness to the town's turbulent and eventful history. Each dynasty has left its mark. Although traces remain of the original palace built in the fourteenth century in the reign of Jayasthiti Malla, the majority of sculptures, monumental doors, courtyards, washing tanks and huge statues date from the sixteenth century.

The palace is constructed around three courtyards — chowks — and no building is more than three storeys high. There are statues on the balconies and erotic sculptures around the walls, discreet yet life-like. On the wrought iron grilles of the balconies the entrails of a sacrificial buffalo are drying out. Outside, at the feet of the stone elephants, a few yards from the golden statue of King Siddhi Narsingh, a legless cripple drags himself along in pursuit of a few coins.

Lifted and carried forward by a fervent crowd, these chariots are brought out only for special occasions.

The third eye

In the streets of Kathmandu, the protective tilaka is applied by a priest.

*Sherpas live in the east
of the country.*

With his spotless turban, neatly trimmed beard, hooked nose and fiery eyes, he commands respect. In the course of the day his wicker basket will be filled with rice and other offerings given by passers-by who will earn favours in Heaven by charitable deeds. Wandering about in Patan, I become aware of the amazing variety of crafts, and the ingenuity of the craftsmen in producing the most marvellous objects out of thin air. In front of me a goldsmith half sitting, half lying on a mat blows down a long metal tube onto the flame of an acetylene torch. As the flame shrinks he directs it onto the centre of a tiny metal lotus flower decorating a ring, creating a bed into which he fixes a garnet or ruby. How can you resist stopping alongside a carpenter sitting cross-legged on one of the steps up to the big tank who is deftly fashioning from a piece of sandalwood a copy of one of the carved windows of the palace. Now and then he stops working, blows away the shavings and smokes his hooka.

Hidden from the crowd, ignored by the hard-pressed guides, is the temple of the « thousand buddhas », a copy of the famous Mahabuddha in the Indian state of Bihar. It is completely covered by row upon row of tiny

The eyes of the Adi Buddha.

terracotta figurines, the sheer number of which produces a positively mesmerising effect. In its shadow children dance in a circle, and two street-traders play Bagh Chal, a complex game in which one player has four tigers and the other twenty sheep which he has to protect. Perhaps it is not just a game after all.

Before leaving Patan I thought it fitting to pay my last respects to Siddhi Narsingh, the creator of all these splendours and riches. Immortal he stands on his column, facing the palace. Behind him a serpent is poised ready to repel an enemy at the first sign of danger. Towards the end of his days Siddhi Narsingh chose to give up his life of ostentatious luxury, and set off, like the Sadhu to beg for his food on the roads of India. What a difference from the destiny of Aniko, the greatest and most skilled of the city's goldsmiths. His glory and his talent were such that Kubla Khan, the great Emperor of China and protector of Marco Polo, invited him to Lhassa in Tibet, then to Peking where he built the Great White Pagoda and created thousands of bronze sculptures, the account of which stirred the imagination of even the Doge of Venice.

When music punctuates prayer

Young bonzes – buddhist priests – must conquer the desire for worldly goods in order to achieve wisdom.

The watchful eye of Buddha

The stupa at Bodhnath is the biggest in Nepal. These tibetans are putting out prayer flags, the wind will carry their message throughout the universe.

*The tilaka is usually
made of cinnabar,
clay, grains of rice,
flower petals, and is worn
on the brow of Hindus.
This third eye is
for seeing the truth.*

At Swayambhunath these bonzes
increase the force of
their prayers
by humming out loud.

The ultimate purification

*In consuming the flesh
of this dead man, Agni,
the God of fire,
frees his soul.*

*Here the spirit transcends matter.
Death is not the end,
but the beginning
of the cycle of reincarnation.*

Home of the Gods

The majesty and mystery of the Himalayas have always fascinated man.
The summit, glaciers, caves and springs are all places of pilgrimage.

In a country where narrow
footpaths provide almost
the only routes of communication,
men's backs are the most
important means of transport.
The porters are usually Sherpa,
whose exceptional stamina belies
their frail appearance.
At an altitude of eighteen
thousand feet or more,
they are quite capable
of marching for over eight
hours a day thus earning
the reputation for having
an extra lung.

Superhuman stamina
is needed to conquer the mountains

Bhadgaon, city of Vishnu

On the road to China, alongside another sacred river, the Hanumante, lies Bhadgaon, the former Bhaktapur, which is supposed to have been founded in the ninth century by the legendary King Ananda Malla. Rival of the other two cities, Bhaktapur has kept a distinct mediaeval character. It was independent until 1768 when the Gurkhas used force to unify the various kingdoms of the valley.

The trolley bus, built — like the road — by the Chinese, costs just a few rupees. It passes through cornfields and through the quarries that supply clay for the brickworks which so darken the sky. In front of the old city is a small, sacred wood which shelters monkeys.

Bhaktapur, dedicated to Vishnu, is lovely at dawn. As the glazed brick roofs start to gleam in the first light under the fine droplets of dispersing mist that still muffles the noises, it seems like a scene from a play, where all the actors move in slow motion. I acquired the habit of taking tea at the Nyatapola, the only café facing the temple of the same name. One cannot help being awed when confronted by it, for it is the tallest temple in Nepal, rising more than one hundred feet into the air. With its five columns, five roofs and five rows of statues standing at intervals around an immense flight of steps, it is a perfect structure, for in Nepal the number five represents, among other things, the four cardinal points plus the zenith.

The second glory of Bhadgaon is no less wondrous : it is the palace built by Rajah Yaksha Malla in 1427 and altered at the end of the seventeen century by King Bhupatindra Malla who reigned for thirty-four years and was an indefatigable builder.

The palace has fifty-five finely carved windows and is famous for its fabulous gold door, considered the apotheosis of the goldsmith's art at that time. It is called Sun Dhoka and provides access to two very beautiful courtyards reserved exclusively for Hindus and guarded by armed Gurkha soldiers. In the city's two museums I have admired the finest collections of the works of Tanka — symbolic painting, fruit of the artist's meditations — and also the best wood carvings designed for the fretwork windows of the palace. They help one to understand the ingenuity necessary in putting up unglazed wooden trellises, which will not only provide protection, but also enable one to see out without being seen.

With its craftsmen and visiting farmers, the town is a surprising mixture of different ways of life. Throughout the dry season thousands of coloured threads hang out to dry in the sun, strung between two poles. They belong to the weavers who live in the neighbouring quarter to the

At the confluence of the rivers Bagmati and Vishumati a pilgrim makes an offering of holy water to Brahma, the sun-God.

Gods everywhere

At dawn, the first act of the day is to pay tribute to the Gods.
This girl is offering grains of rice, flower petals and cinnabar to Buddha.

potters. With a certain daring, these latter stack up around their shops huge glazed platters, finely decorated plates and all sorts of kitchen receptacles. A woman seated in the square in front of a temple sifts rice between her fingers, separating the grains from bits of straw which fly about in the wind and stick to the wet bodies of young children washing themselves on their doorsteps. A buffalo passes, dragging at its neck a lump of wood to stop it from running off too quickly. Near the well, spread out on mats to dry in the sun, is *gundruk,* the grass used for making soup. It is chopped finely then scalded in boiling water and left to ferment in earthenware pots with straw stoppers.

The street in which I stand, Kuache, changes its name three or four times over a short distance, and at each change I am in a different century. I walk past beautiful houses which have just been renovated and open onto little courtyards. The happy laughter of women and children filters down from the balconies. Cooking smells escape from all around. Stalls are stocked with all sorts of spices whose reds, oranges and yellows reflect the colours of the temples. Sitting against the wall, mothers surrounded by their offspring work quickly at strange octagonal-shaped spinning wheels, chewing betel.

This tranquility that I love to experience contrasts strongly with the decor of the Dattatreya, a temple consecrated to Vishnu, which, legend has it, was built with the wood from a single tree. Dattatreya is held as the creator of knowledge and of the most mysterious of Tantric rites. After seeing so very many temples, carvings and people, the desire to go off in search of peaceful paddyfields, meadows and mountains, overwhelms me. A few miles to the north of the town there is a very special sanctuary, Changu Narayan, situated three thousand feet up on one of the loveliest hills in the entire valley. After the Nagarkot road I have to walk for nearly two hours before reaching the temple. For the whole length of this trip, as far as the eye can see, the terraces of the green striped paddyfields stretch out around the hills. A path leads off to the right, used by the villagers and their herds. The air is fresher, you can see and hear for miles. After the bad road that leads to a military station painted white, you round the bend, and at last there it is — proud, majestic, imperial, legendary : Mount Everest. It dominates the whole countryside and fills the horizon to the west where the Himalayas unfold and reveal their jewels, the Dhaulagiri and the beautiful peak of Annapurna.

Agriculture is Nepal's main economic activity, although cultivated land represents no more than ten per cent of the country.

Relaxation

One of the precious moments of the day, often accompanied by the smoking of a hooka.

A rural scene of Bhadgaon.

*Fifty per cent of the cereals
produced in the Kathmandu
valley are exported to India
in exchange for manufactured goods.*

the gardens of the roof of the world

If you wish to form a complete picture of the country, it is essential to get away from the towns and the valley and make for either the mountains or the plains of the Terai. As the monsoon is now behind us, and it will be fine from November until March, let us start with the Terai and its animal reserves, where tigers, leopards and the one-horned rhinoceros roam freely.

Not so long ago, less than twenty years in fact, the region was still declared a disaster area, where flooded rivers carried away whole villages and where cobras, scorpions and disease-carrying mosquitos prevented any access whatever. Now the situation has completely changed. With the drying out of the marsh and the disappearance of malaria, the alluvial plain has been opened up to marsh culture and even to tourism. Roads have been built and aerodromes constructed ; even the elephants from a luxury camp in the middle of Chitwan National Park have been pressed into service, collecting passengers straight from the runway as they disembark from the twin-engined planes which shuttle between Kathmandu and Meghauli.

One of the best ways of getting to know the real heart of the country, which you may miss if you stick to the dusty roads, is to descend the rapids

A Newar wearing a traditional topi on his head.

and rivers of the Himalayas, a route first introduced by a few sporting enthusiasts. Setting off from the town centre in the early hours of the morning, the mini-bus has some difficulty at first in making its way through the crowds of porters converging on the capital from all sides. Once past the first police control point, on the Pokhara road, our speed increases substantially until we are averaging twenty miles an hour, a pretty good performance, thanks to the driver, who, in true Nepalese fashion, knows no fear. Overtaking on narrow, precipitous roads and at blind corners is all part of the fun. Vultures fly off above us as we skirt the mountainside with the horn permanently pressed. The bus stops near a little village on the river Trisuli. It is wide, green and shallow at this time of year, and flows between two vertical rock faces linked by a long suspension bridge. Here the atmosphere changes. With the first strokes of the oars the mood is set ; the few traces of the modern world completely vanish, and we see almost another country, one which has barely changed over the centuries. Villages appear on the sides of the valley, children run amidst the rocks shouting and waving their arms. Often they are quite naked, and they chase after monkeys that laze in the sun. Lowing buffalo pull the plough along the furrows of the terraces. Woodmen try to salvage floating driftwood from the current. Life on the riverbanks is quite different. Those who live there generally refuse all direct contact with the outside world. Not even the gold prospectors, busy washing and sifting the grit from the creeks in a crude sieve, raise their heads as we pass by.

The descent of the Trisuli takes three days, broken by the overnight stops, with campfires on untouched beaches. Children appear out of the dark and gather round the logs. Sometimes they dance, but often they are silent, attentive and helpful. Then at first light they slip away, taking food with them.

Forests and mountains gradually give way to cultivated plains. The straw roofs of huts stick up out of the cornfields. At the confluence of the Trisuli and the Kali Gandaki, the swollen waters become the Narayani River, and a modest sanctuary marks the spot. Banners flutter in the wind, prayer flags twist round ropes thrown from tree to tree. Floral garlands bob along with the current that will take them to the Ganges. A few yards above the river bed, on a rocky spur, a man naked from the waist up, hirsuit and bearded, meditates silently. This is Crazy Baba, a mystic who has progressively cut off his fingers, his hand, his forearm and the rest of his arm as a protest against the violence of the world.

A sizeable crowd comes to see him each day, and both his audience and the seething waters carry off the echo of his slightest gesture as far as Benares, holy city of India.

Spirals of smoke rise up towards the south. On a funeral pyre a body burns. Friends and relations attend the cremation. Barely ten feet away a driver is washing down his lorry, which stands up to its axles in the river, now flowing gently and listlessly since we have left the mountains. Brahmani ducks, white and orange, fly off at our approach.

On the banks wild peacocks spread their tails. They need fear nothing, for they are sacred. Monkeys watch us, and in a hollow of warm sand gavials (a species of crocodile in danger of becoming extinct) sleep with one eye always open. At the slightest suspicious sound they dive into the river with amazing speed until nothing can be seen of them but two nostrils. Birds that were hushed for a moment recommence their singing and deer come out of the forest. A hog rummages in the roots of a fromager. Without

In front of Simba-Sattal, the Shivaic oratory, the faithful gather to make offerings.

really noticing I have just crossed the boundary of the National Park.

Chitwan National Park shelters over four hundred different species of birds and it seems as though they have all come together to welcome us. But the most enchanting sight is of the freshwater dolphins, leaping up at us and wickedly spraying us with water.

It is very early in the morning and the sun's rays are struggling to penetrate the mist. Moisture trickles from the roofs, falling in heavy drops onto the balconies. All at once I hear sounds from the hidden path behind the wooden buildings of the camp : a slow, heavy tread, the crashing of the undergrowth and the creaking of leather. An enormous form appears, trunk lifted, ears flapping about the legs of the *mahout* (elephant keeper) perched on its back. The docile animal then takes up position beneath a ledge that allows for easy access to and from the saddle without its having to kneel.

The elephant moves with a slow and swinging gait. It feels strange at first though in no way unpleasant. Then on its master's orders it leaves the path and heads for the long grass, demonstrating astounding agility as it moves silently over the steepest slopes. After a short while fresh rhinoceros tracks are spotted, whether by the *mahout* or his charge I am not sure. We are off in pursuit, amidst splintering bamboo and the rustling of the grasses that surround us, with the occasional dry crack of dead branches broken by a mischievious trunk.

Our decidedly uncooperative rhinoceros burrows deeper into the undergrowth, grunting and blowing, then after allowing us a glimpse of grey wrinkled hide, vanishes again from sight. When it eventually stops to fix us with its gaze, its stumpy ears all quivering, the elephant will be perfectly composed and ready for the confrontation.

In the distance the snow-capped mountains stand out against the clear blue sky. Only this sight distinguishes the plain of Terai from the African savannah grassland. Faced with the spectacle I feel an irresistible urge to climb to the « roof of the world » as soon as I can.

Pokhara is the traditional departure point for trips to the valleys of Thakkola and Muktinath, and for expeditions into the Annapurna range. The valley of Pokhara lies in the centre of the country, some 27 000 feet up, and enjoys a sub-tropical climate and characteristic range of vegetation all the more astonishing considering its situation at the foot of those fabulous peaks. To my great surprise, I discover in the course of my walks, whole fields of orange and lemon trees in blossom, banana trees and hedges of euphorbia edging the paddyfields. Blue lakes reflect the eternal peaks, boats glide towards miniature temples perched on little green islands. Wild flowers quiver in the spray from the falls.

With the coming of the road and the aerodrome, the little town has lost its mythical aura, but remains the base for the finest treks in the world. There are treks to the Kubhine pass, where numb with cold but happy, I watch the sun rise over Annapurna. The summit of Pacbahaiya, overlooking lakes Bagna and Rupa, is a good place to stop for a moment's meditation. Other slopes provide wonderful three-week long adventures, walking all over the range with spectacular views over the whole of the Himalayas. As the altitude increases, the scenery changes. On the higher slopes meadows and yak pastures give way to masses of flowering rhododendron, some of which are enormous specimens. Higher yet, on the Muktinath side, there is nothing but the rocks where thickly muffled pilgrims search with infinite patience for shaligrams, the black and fossilised amonites that are one of the reincarnated forms of Vishnu.

Source of life

Water is a threefold symbol : source of life, means of purification and substance of regeneration. It is the basic element of bodily and spiritual existence.

*The streets bear witness
to the easy co-existence...*

*... of the sacred
and the profane.*

The quintessence of Newar art

*The Shiva-Parvati mandir
with its carved beams
and wooden trellises is a remarkable
example of Newar architecture.*

*Built in the eighteenth century,
this is the most famous
temple in Kathmandu.*

The children of God

*With their heads shaved and in a new set of clothes,
the young Hindus take part in an initiation ceremony.*

The protector of the home

The good and indispensable elephant-featured Ganesh is a friendly presence protecting every home. He chose to live on Ganesh Himal, one of the Himalayas' most beautiful peaks.

The bull, a symbol of plenty and strength, is respected throughout Asia...

... Because of its special qualities it is considered worthy of being sacrificed to the Gods.

Strength and sacrifice

Rice, coins and flowers are presented at one of the many shrines.

Wearing the mark of Shiva.

Beneath the roof of the world

Eleven thousand two hundred feet up, Namche Bazar is the last stage before the famous Thyangboche monastery at the foot of mount Everest.

earthly Gods

Nepal is traditionally a place of asylum, and its inhabitants have always practised religious tolerance, as is evident everywhere today. As a result, and extraordinary variety of feast days punctuates the year, particularly since several calendars are used concurrently.

It is *Loshar,* the Tibetan New Year, when everyone is happy and glad to be alive. There are joyful reunions and celebrations among the thousands of people that have come down from the mountains and out of the refugee camps. They arrive in groups, smiling, wearing their finest clothes and chewing betel. They prostrate themselves in waves before the great yellow Buddhas that line the flight of three hundred steps leading to the superb stupa of Swayambhunath. They are dressed in finely embroidered leather jackets, and wear tall woollen hats whose flaps only half cover their ears to reveal big gold ear-rings with twisted strands framing a blue stone. Moving round the bonfires, they place little statues carved out of clay on the altars.

The women pause to show off their big chased copper hair combs while children jostle around the ice-cream sellers. Tomorrow, after a late night of festivities, they will go to Bodhnath, the biggest stupa in all Nepal.

This building, the surface area of each level decreasing with its height, is surrounded by a circular area edged by a brick wall which has one hundred and forty-seven niches for prayer wheels. « Om Mani Padme Hum », they grind continuously. Monks join in with the mountain people distinguished by their long hair and big woollen robes. Together they finger their beads and turn small, finely carved prayer wheels with supple wrist movements.

Higher up on the steps, the crowd is in the process of changing the hundreds of brightly coloured prayer flags flapping in the wind, right up to the golden crown that overhangs the gigantic eyes of the red, blue and white painted Buddhas on each side of the square tower.

Rice is tossed in the air and sticks of incense are burned.

A Sherpa child.

A moment of magic

Their joy and wonder at anything magical make the Nepalese and enthusiastic and eager audience.

*Acrobats, jugglers and magicians
practise their simple arts…*

... to the great joy
of the public.

Power brought to heel

The centuries old team of mahout and elephant consumate the union of strength and intelligence.

*In the depths of Chitwan National Park
the one-horned rhinoceros is becoming
more and more scarce.*

*As Atlas in the west,
so the elephant in the
east bears the world
on its back.*

Nyatapola is supposed to have been the model for the pagodas of China.

The stupa − part shrine, part commemorative monument − is the centre of all spiritual activity. It is built in the shape of a hemisphere supported on a raised flat base.

Shrines provide a link with heaven

*A group of Sherpas
on the footpaths
of Mount Everest.*

Monks blow into big trumpets that resound and re-echo. The Lamas' heads
of saffron hair bow down, hands are joined, there are prayers and hopes
amidst the crackling fires.

But not all the festivals are so happy and carefree. The most important, Dasain, which lasts for ten days in October, commemorates the victory
of Durga (one of the forms of the goddess Kali or Taleju, protector of the
Kings of Nepal), against Mahisasura, the buffalo demon.

The first days of the Dasain rites are essentially celebrated in the
family, and only the men are allowed to enter the alcove for the Kalash, a
magic flask containing the energy of Durga. Whereas the nights are
reserved for bathing, which the faithful must do either in the rivers or in the
huge water tanks that are to be found in every town, during the day the
people walk about the streets and go to the markets, where thousands of
buffalo, sheep, cockerel and guinea-fowl are assembled. Everyone chooses
a beast for the sacrifice.

During the night preceding the ninth day, the bells of the temples start
to ring out all over the country and the sacrificing begins. Cockerel and
goats have their throats slit beside the vehicles that have brought the faithful

*Khumbe Yula is the eternal home
of the Bhudda of the Sherpas.*

to the religious places. Military bands play uninterrupted to encourage the Kasai who must behead with a single stroke each of the hundred and eight buffalo in the courtyard of Kathmandu's old palace. The skins are dragged around a column and the priests place the heads in the sanctuary of the Kumari, where they will act as a test of her courage. The head of every household takes out his weapons, his tools and the seed to be sown in the fields. He pours a little water into the ears of the animal to be sacrificed, and when it shakes its head — the sign of approval — the sword falls. The same ritual is being observed all over the country outside all the principal sanctuaries ; even at the airport a goat is sacrificed in front of the standing planes.

The tenth and final day is for public rejoicing. The members of each community get together for a big reconciliation. They call on their elders and their parents to receive the *tilaka* on their foreheads. The canons are fired thirty one times to announce that the King too has received Durga's blessing, and in the streets Newar priests march waving their swords, with which they sometimes touch a passer-by informing him that he is soon to fall gravely ill, or perhaps even die.

One of the many rivers
of Sagarmatha National Park.

Along the border of China
and Nepal the Himalayas have
forty peaks of over 21000 feet
which continue to grow higher
with the pressure of the earth's movements.

Lake of legends

At the foot Annapurna an atmosphere of serenity surrounds the lakes of Pokhara.

Pashupati, lord of the animals

When a man's life draws to its close and he is on the point of death, he is laid on the ground and his whole family gathers round him, each member pouring a little water into his mouth. Then without delay the dying man is carried to the edge of the River Bagmati. To be cremated on the Ghats, alongside the river at Pashupatinath, remains the last wish of every fervent Hindu. Many old people are brought here to end their days. Pashupatinath is one of the most ancient Nepalese sanctuaries and the goal of many different pilgrimages each year. The most amazing is the gathering of Sadhu who come on foot from Benares and from all over India. More than twenty thousand of them have made this pilgrimage, which takes several months, but what is time to one who has come to worship Shiva, represented here in his gentlest guise as the herdsman Pashupati.

From first light this morning there are funeral processions one after another on the Ghats. They are led by a man throwing coins and grains of rice every ten paces. Friends follow, along with members of the family and priests who surround the bamboo litter and the body wrapped in a shroud. The crowd moves silently ; there is no weeping and no moaning, only a great dignity and reserve in their bearing.

When the funeral pyre is ready — only the very well-off families can still offer sandalwood — the eldest son, or a close male friend sets light to a little net smeared with butter laid on the mouth of the dead man. Tulsi leaves, camphor and melted butter have been placed among the logs and grains of rice sprinkled on the shroud. They are supposed to ease the journey which leads to a new cycle of existence.

When the all-consuming flames subside the ashes and other remains will be scattered on the waters of the Bagmati.

The lasting impression is of the serenity of this place, of its prayers and of a faith that is almost tangible, awing visitors into silence. Entry to the temple is forbidden to non-Hindus, and so I watch from the other side of the Bagmati, from the hill overlooking the shrines with their little white bell towers, and admire the three gilded roofs that have been here for nearly three centuries.

Further up again, in the shade of the trees where a few monkeys are playing, is a group of Sadhu. Three red stripes are painted on their brows, they have long hair and dusty bare feet, they are furnished with a begging bowl and a stick in the shape of a trident. They represent the past and the future. They are at one with God. They have journeyed hundreds of miles in search of the absolute. In Nepal they have found it.

Namaste
– Farewell –

ACKNOWLEDGEMENTS

Pierre Toutain
and Temps de Pose Editions
would particularly like
to thank the following :

In Paris

The Ambassador of Nepal
M. Thapa, Nepalese embassy
M. Georges Lebrec, President of the France-Nepal Association
Mme Marie-Clothilde Debieuvre and
M. Lorrain Kressman - Air France press office

Mme Nicole Donnat
M. Rémi Berli
Mlle Béatrice Soulas
Mme Marie-Hélène Soulas
M. & Mme Jacques Moiroux
Kodak
Canon

Canon

In London
Mr John Cumming, The Print Room, 37, Museum Street, London WC1
Ms Sue Jenkins

In New Delhi
Mr R. Khare, Air France

In Nepal
Mr Utpal Sengupta, manager of the Shangrila Hotel

HOTEL
SHANGRILA
Kathmandu

Yeti Travels
Tiger Tops
Air France, Kathmandu
Indian Airlines

For their contribution
to the production of this book.

All photographs were taken using Kodachrome 64 film.